The Place Where God Dwells

An Introduction to Church Architecture in Asia

Masao Takenaka

Christian Conference of Asia
and
Asian Christian Art Association
in association with Pace Publishing

The Place Where God Dwells
First published 1995:

Christian Conference of Asia,
96 2nd District, Paktin Village
Meitin Road, Shatin N.T.
Hong Kong

and
Asian Christian Art Association,
Kansai Seminar House,
23 Takenouchi-cho, Ichijoji,
Sakyo-ku, Kyoto 606, Japan

in associationwith:
Pace Publishing,
P.O. Box 15.774,
Auckland 1007, New Zealand.

Printed by Clearcut Printing Co. Ltd., Hong Kong.

ISBN: 0.9597971-5-7

Contents

About the Title:

The title of this publication, *The Place Where God Dwells*, derives from the word "Devasthanaya". In the language of the Sinhala people of Sri Lanka, "Devasthanaya" means "God's Place" or "God's House".

This literal translation has been given a more poetic expression in order to embrace the emotion and faith which are part of any religious belief.

Of course God does not dwell only in religious buildings. God dwells in fields and mountains and in every small village. And God dwells in the heart of the believer wherever that person might be.

The construction of churches and temples is a visible expression of human faith and worship. In every langauge such buildings are recognised as centres of faith and described as "the house of God" or "God's dwelling place".

Preface

One of the important priorities of the Christian Conference of Asia (CCA) is the promotion of Asian Christian spirituality expressed in architecture, arts, church music and theology. These arts, music and theology are not only serving the needs and renewal of Asian churches but they are also contributing to the wider ecumenical world.

In 1963 the East Asia Christian Conference (the present Christian Conference of Asia) published the *EACC Hymnal*. This book has been printed several times and even today churches and publishers around the world continue to ask CCA's permission to reproduce hymns from *CCA Hymnal*. In 1990, in cooperation with the Asian Institute for Liturgy and Music, CCA published a new CCA Hymnal titled *Sound the Bamboo*, which was jointly edited by Fr. James Minchin, Prof. I-to Loh and Dr. Francisco Feliciano.

Asian Christian art is found in churches, homes and museums around the world. The first milestone in CCA's work of introducing and promoting Asian Christian art was the book *Christian Art in Asia*, jointly published by the Christian Conference of Asia and Kyo Bun Kwan, Tokyo in 1975. The book was edited by Dr. Masao Takenaka, professor of theology and social ethics at Doshisha University, Kyoto with support from Rev. Ron O'Grady, then Associate General Secretary of the Life and Action Unit of CCA.

The work of introducing Christian art in Asia was continued by the Asian Christian Art Association through its quarterly magazine, *Image*. In 1991, *The Bible Through Asian Eyes*, edited by Prof. Masao Takenaka and Rev. Ron O'Grady, was launched at Canberra during the Seventh General Assembly of the World Council of Churches.

Some years ago questions relating to the architecture of churches in Asia were raised within the CCA. Should churches reflect an indigenous expression of Christianity and if they do, can they remain relevant in a rapidly changing world? To what extent have experiments at indigenisation been successful? Does church architecture have any influence on the types of worship and liturgy and on the relationship of the church with the community?

In response to these questions, Dr Judo Poerwowidagdo, a theologian from Indonesia and Mr Ken Hassall, an architect from Australia, travelled around Asia at the request of the CCA. They visited churches and chapels in a number of places and their preliminary report was published in *Image* (No. 7 March 1981), the Asian Christian Art Association's quarterly magazine.

The ultimate goal was to produce a book on church architecture in Asia and this initial research was a good beginning. But Asia is a wide geographic area with a great diversity of cultures and it was realised that additional material would be required to give a more comprehensive picture, so the publication of a book was delayed.

Time has passed and now it is felt that it is better to use what material we have been able to gather together in the interim, incomplete though it still may be, rather than delay publication indefinitely. We recognise the limitations of the material in representation of countries and of different denominations of the Christian faith. But we bring this book to birth in the hope that it will stimulate the thinking of Christians in Asia as they contemplate their present places of worship and consider future building projects.

Dr Masao Takenaka, professor of Ethics at Doshisha University and honorary president of the Asian Christian Art Association, has written the introductory text.

Editing of the materials and design and layout of the book are the work of Alison O'Grady, currently editor of *Image,* the magazine of the Asian Christian Art Association.

Grateful thanks and appreciation are extended to those organisations which have generously provided support for this project; they include the Church of Sweden Mission, Evangelisches Missionswerk in Deutschland, Missio in Germany and Kyo Bun Kwan in Japan.

I feel honoured to write the preface to this book on Christian architecture in Asia and trust that readers will find it a useful and informative resource.

Tosh Arai
Associate General Secretary,
Christian Conference of Asia.

The Place Where God Dwells

1 The Body of Christ in Asia

Structural Embodiment of Christ

The word "Church" has many connotations in Christian theology and there have been a variety of interpretations and expressions of the church throughout the Christian era. In his book *Images of the Church in the New Testament*, Paul Minear claims there are over eighty images of the church in the New Testament.

This plurality of the images of the Church does not mean that there is no basic integrating foundation. People cannot create another image of the church according to their own preference. One orchestra has a variety of instruments with their distinctive sounds but there is the central theme running through the orchestra.

The central theme in the New Testament is Jesus Christ, his life and ministry, his death and resurrection. There are various accounts and different accents in its interpretation and expression but there is a cornerstone upon which to build the house of God: "See, I am laying in Zion a stone, a cornerstone chosen and precious; and whoever believes on him will not be put to shame." (1 Peter 2:6)

Paul Minear, while depicting the variety of images of the church in the New Testament, distinguishes the major images and the minor images of the church. He depicts one of the major key images of the body of Christ as follows:

"We have now completed the second stage of our project, having reviewed the uses of some eighty analogies and designations for Christian community in the New Testament. Only one major configuration of thought awaits exploration - that which oscillates around three terms; body, members, head."[1]

The image of the church as expressed in terms of the body of Christ in the world is a powerful image which contains profound meaning in the contemporary ecclesiology in Asia. The church consists of the people of God who become part of the body of Christ by accepting "Jesus Christ as God and

The Body of Christ, Bagong Kussudiardja, Indonesia.

Saviour according to Holy Scripture thus to glorify the Father, Son and Holy Spirit." (The basis of the World Council of Churches)

As the event of incarnation is the manifestation of God in human form in time and place, the church exists in history and in locality. It is a universal community and, at the same time, it is a local manifestation of the body of Christ. It is not the perfect community of God without spot and wrinkle (Ephesians 5:27) yet it is the community which transforms and renews itself by accepting the Word of God and the divine body and blood. (1 Corinthians 11:24-25) It is a human community which is called to be God's people by following the steps of Christ in the world. (1 Peter 2:9-12)

It is the earthly community participating in the worldly suffering and struggle and also the community of hope anticipating the ultimate liberation and the final consummation. It is a visible earthly vessel to signify and point out the eternal life which works through it.

In this book we are concerned about how the church exists as the body of Christ in Asia through the medium of architecture. The word architecture consists of two words: 'arch' which means primary and 'tecture' which indicates technological structure. Thus, architecture means the basic structure. In this sense, church architecture in Asia means the basic structure of the body of Christ in Asia.

Historical Tradition

The church is the historical embodiment of Christ. One of the strengths of the Christian church is that the church as the historical institution formulated distinctive styles of church building in response to the challenging demands of each period. We appreciate the rich heritage of church architecture which inspires us to be creative in the context of each place and time.

We recognise the historical period, the cultural context and the natural environment in which the church lived but we do not wish to imitate the particular style and form. We are stimulated by the fact that with devotion and concentrated effort people in each period have wrestled to formulate their own distinctive style of church architecture which will be the embodiment of Christ - from the catacomb period and Basilica style, through Byzantine and Romanesque form to Gothic expression, reformed and colonial style. These former styles challenge us to find our own contextual creative embodiment of Christ in Asia.

One example from the church architecture of Romania will illustrate this point. At the invitation of the Romanian Orthodox Church I had the privilege to visit some churches and monasteries in Tschava, the northeast region of Romania. Some of the churches are large and others are small but each fits the natural environment. All are decorated inside and outside with icons and pictorial designs utilising the folk art of the people. These churches stand quietly in the countryside, indicating the artistic and indigenous expression of the body of Christ in Romanian context. Most of the pictures are from Biblical scenes such as the creation and fall, the annunciation and incarnation, the ministry of Christ leading towards the cross and the resurrection and ascension.

I could not identify some figures placed alongside the Biblical prophets such as Isaiah and Jeremiah. "Who are they?" I asked and my Romanian friend replied, "They are Greek philosophers." Socrates, Plato, Pythagoras and Aristotle are depicted on the wall of the church. As Thomas Aquinas incorporated the philosophy of Aristotle into his theological structure, so those pictures testify to the process of acculturation taking place over the centuries.

Orthodox Church, Romania.

Dr. D.T. Niles once remarked, "We, the churches in Asia, confront two temptations; one is syncretism and the other is ghettoism and the latter is stronger."

When I carefully observed some of the walls of the Romanian church I noticed the design of three ropes which became one through the process of interaction. This is certainly the expression of the Trinitarian faith of the daily life of the cattle-raising people of the area.

The roof of the chapel is not steep like those churches of Gothic design but soft and round, giving a feeling of cosmic harmony with the acknowledgement of Christ as pantocrator under whose light the liturgy is celebrated. Many churches are located on a hillside or in the middle of a valley surrounded by low mountains and seem to fit in with the change of four seasons.

Knowing that these churches are the product of different historical and social circumstances we should not imitate or transform their forms and style but they challenge the Asian churches to wrestle with the issue of acculturation and the development of indigenous forms of church buildings.

Colonial Heritage

With few exceptions, most of the churches in Asia are the product of the Western missionary movement, beginning with the period of geographic discovery by explorer Vasco da Gama and the Catholic missionary movement led by men like Francis Xavier who made strenuous efforts to bring the seed of the gospel to Asian soil in the sixteenth century. Then during the period of colonisation, along with Western civilisation and way of life came the introduction to Asia of Christianity through the modern missionary movement from the West.

While appreciating the devotion and commitment of the missionaries who courageously preached the gospel and helped to found the churches in Asia, this was nevertheless the expansion of 'Western' Christianity. Certainly some of the missionaries were farsighted enough to advocate and encourage the indigenous expression of Christian faith from an early stage but generally Western forms of church structure and church architecture were transplanted in Asia. Moreover, many Asian churches at that time not only imported Western architectural styles for their buildings but also the interior decoration and atmosphere was often dominated by colonial mentality.

During this period, due to the fear of idolatry, many Protestant church buildings in Asia focussed on the pulpit. Because of the emphasis on preaching the word of God, any consideration of creative forms of artistic expression was seldom pursued and usually was entirely neglected. Consequently, many Asians accustomed to appreciate the artistic atmosphere of traditional Asian religions feel Christian church buildings are more like Western lecture halls rather than places which promote a religious atmosphere for ordinary Asian people.

Two positive factors in regard to church building in this period need to be registered. One is that due to the missionary movement, many Asian churches were located in a strategic place within the city or the country. This shows that in many cases churches at that time had support from the Western mission and some even received favour from the colonial government. As a result, Christian churches in many parts of Asia possess valuable property in the city and country. Today, following the transformation of the administrative work of the church, Asian church leaders are challenged to make responsible use of the precious property for the up-building of the body of Christ in Asia.

Another positive note during the missionary period is that despite the general trend of Westernisation, we recognise several pioneering people, both Western and national leaders, who attempted to formulate Asian expression utilising indigenous materials and sensitivity. An example is the Episcopal church building in the heart of Nara, the old capital city of Japan which was built in 1930 (see p.66)

Post-War Struggle

After World War II a new climate developed in Asia. With the establishment of new independent states most churches in Asia also gained self-government and self-identity. In 1957 in the town of Prapat, Indonesia, the churches in Asia prepared for the establishment of a regional fellowship known as the East Asia Christian Conference (EACC) which had its Inaugural Assembly in Kuala Lumpur in May 1959.

One of the most significant meetings in the initial days of the EACC was the consultation on confessing the faith in Asia held in Hong Kong, October 26 - November 3, 1966. This was the first time that EACC expressed a conmprehensive theological statement of Christian faith in an Asian context put together by Asian church leaders and creative theologians. The statement issued by the consultation called "Confessing the Faith in Asia Today" still provides the basic perspective for the Asian church.[2]

Prof. Masao Takenaka answers questions following his lecture at the Inaugural Assembly of the EACC, May 14-24 1959, Kuala Lumpur, Malaysia. Dr. David Moses is presiding.

The report of the section on culture, after examining the criteria of confession, deals with the basic attitude to culture as follows:

"The gospel enables Christians as well as the Church to live joyfully, though not uncritically, in that culture into which they are born and which itself is a part of God's creative gift to people. The churches in Asia cannot truly be confessing churches as long as they remain societies apart from mainstream and common life of Asian nations. Both the churches and their setting of culture are under his lordship." Further, the statement listed five responsibilities of Asian churches as they relate themselves to Asian culture: i) the responsibility to learn, ii) the responsibility to interpret, iii) the responsibility to belong, iv) the responsibility to mediate and v) the responsibility to be creative.[3]

Based on this approach, in the field of church hymnology the *EACC Hymnal*[4] was published in 1963 and a further edition published in 1990 with the title *Sound the Bamboo*[5]. In the field of visual art, *Christian Art in Asia*[6] published in 1975 and *The Bible Through Asian Eyes*[7] published in 1991 were further indications to show the effort of Asian Christians to confess the faith in a cultural context.

One reason why the concern over architecture took some time to develop was the fact that in the post-war period churches were pressed by the immediate tasks of emerging nations. Also, the churches needed more time to concentrate their energies to engage with the church building which requires much more consolidated joint work with considerable capital investment.

Recent Renewal

In the past fifteen years we have seen increasing demand for the development of new church building in Asia, partly due to the fact that many old churches have been decaying and must be reconstructed and partly because there is new awareness and interest in Asian identity and creativity in the expression of Christian faith.

One may say that what was discussed and stated at the EACC consultation in Hong Kong in 1966 in relation to Asian culture became more widely the concern of Asian churches. In the immediate post-war period the churches were confronted with immediate day-by-day needs and when they constructed a church building they either took the form of the Western church or built the church in terms of expediency rather than involving themselves in a joint effort to search for appropriate structures for the church in Asia.

One concrete example from the Japanese situation will illustrate this point. Many churches were built in the post-war period in Japan and many books published on Western church buildings, both historical surveys and also on particular churches or cathedrals. Yet there was not a single book published covering theology, history and practical guides on church architecture in Japan until 1985, when the first such comprehensive book[8] was published.

It is significant to note that in the book not only Orthodox, Catholic and Protestant theologians contributed articles but also two professional architects made contributions by introducing such subjects as "A History of Church Building Prewar Period and Postwar Period in Japan" and "The Problems of Church Building Today in Japan from an Architect's Point of View".

Similarly in India artists and church leaders are jointly involved in an ecumenical search for the relevant modern expression of church in an Indian context.[9]

In this sense I believe this book is a timely publication for Asian churches as they search for their own form of church building in the midst of the cultural renaissance in Asia.

II Church in Space

Theology of Space (topos)

On the top of the Reformed Church in Switzerland we often see the symbol of the cock which indicates the time of awakening and it is not unusual to find a clock on the tower of the church. It shows that Western churches are very time and history oriented. In Asia we cannot overlook the historical dimension of church but we need to take nature into our consideration when we construct church buildings. We need to develop the consideration of space in our church architecture in Asia.

In Genesis we learn that God created heaven and earth and put human beings in the garden as the responsible keepers (Genesis 1 and 2). As we are called to be involved in history, equally we are called to responsible participation in nature. In this connection, it is important to see the meaning of 'Shakkei' in the realm of Japanese architecture. 'Shakkei' means literally 'to borrow the scenery'. It indicates imaginative use of nature by borrowing the scenery which belongs to others in such a way that it looks like one's own back yard. In other words, it is creative use of the landscape by arranging the architecture to fit in the environment.[10]

This is a very useful and creative method, particularly in a country where space is so limited. Consider the case of the Episcopal Church in Nara, where the architect creatively used the moutain of Mikasa as if it is the back yard of the church. If the natural environment is part of God's creation, it is important to consider the way in which to find fitting participation in the environment for the church building.

Episcopal Church, Nara, Japan.

Meaning of 'Ma' (in-between)

A basic way to count space in north east Asia is 'ma' which literally means 'in between'. In Japanese language, the effort to divide space into certain functional rooms is called madori - to allocate the space in between. Thus the guest room is called kyakuma (guest space), the living room is i-ma (space of living), the window is called mado (the door in between). This indicates the importance of recognising the space in between other space.

What does it mean in our church architecture in Asia? If

the church is the place to worship God and is also the meeting place of God and human beings, there must be a special symbolic space of holiness. In the ordinary Japanese house there is the space called tokonoma which is the special space to hang the picture and to set the flower arrangement to admire the spirit of the coming season.

Similarly, there should be a holy place set apart to symbolise the encounter between time and eternity. Moses took off his shoes when he saw the burning bush since this place was the holy place where God revealed himself in the midst of the wilderness. (Exodus 3:5) We need to have a special space of holy emptiness in our church.

Work '86, Yi Choon Ki, Korea.

Circle and Harmony

For the space of church to express symbolically the spirit of Christian community which is manifested in the spirit of love and harmony, it is helpful to take the shape of circle rather than an antagonistic position. Yi Choon Ki, one of the creative modern Korean artists, has expressed the cosmic circle with the four colours which correspond with four seasons as well as four symbolic animals. The colour of blue indicates spring and dragon; the colour of red is for summer and sparrow; the colour of white represents autumn and tiger; and the colour of black is winter and reptile.

We believe the spirit of harmony and love can be filled in the body of Christ as promised in the prophecy of Isaiah.[11] In this sense, to promote an atmosphere of harmony and mutual acceptance it is preferable to have the seating arrangement of the church in a circle rather than in an antagonistic and monological way. Also, in accordance with the tradition of many Asian countries, we may sit on the floor without using the chair at all. The space of the church should promote the spirit of mutual sharing and common participation in life which is given by Christ.

Irregularity is Beautiful

Whereas rational and symmetrical beauty was appreciated in the Western concept of excellence as advocated by Jonathan Edwards[12], in Asia we appreciate irregular use of space. Soetsu Yanagi, one of the outstanding philosophers of the folk art movement said:

"The irregular is in a sense something to which all who pursue true beauty resort. But primitive art from Africa, the Americas and the South Seas was an astonishing revelation and had a magnetic effect on artists like Picasso and Matisse. Such art, as nothing else, freely expressed the beauty of deformation, of the irregular, that they sought. This resuscitation from primitive sources surely ranks with the revelation afforded by the colour prints of Japan in the late nineteenth and early twentieth century."[13]

In the gardens of Versailles in France, beauty is seen through the symmetrically designed space in which flower and grass are equally arranged side by side. In the garden of Katsura palace in Japan, nothing is symmetrical. The stones are arranged irregularly on the green moss which also forms an irregular shape. I believe both are beautiful but in the Asian church I would prefer that we continue to appreciate irregular design over regular - since each individual creature has a unique and distinctive shape - and yet maintain unity in harmony as a whole.

Open Space

The church is not a closed community. It is an open community: open to the dimension of eternity and also open to the horizon of humanity. In this sense, the gate has a very significant role to play. It signifies the space to enter into the temple to meet God and, at the same time, indicates the open space to go out from in order to participate in Christ's work in the world.

This rhythm of coming in and going out is an indispensible movement of the body of Christ, just as we breath in and out in our bodily movement. Every one who visits a Shinto shrine in Japan notices the beautiful gate (torii) through which entry is gained into the temple. The Psalmist also expressed the religious conviction that God protects and sustains us as we are going out and coming in (Psalm 121:8). In the New Testament, Christ encourages us to enter through the narrow gate (Matthew 7:13) and also declared "I am the gate for the sheep." (John 10:7)

Transformation

This openness is illustrated strikingly in the church at Blimbingsari in Bali, Indonesia which I believe is one of the most remarkable examples of indigenous church architecture in Asia. (see page 102) The church takes rich Balinese cultural heritages in spacial arrangement and architectural style and transforms the old to bring something new. It has a clearly defined Christian orientation and expression. Blimbingsari Church is situated in a small village in the north west of Bali about 100 kilometres from the city of Denpasar. Arriving there one is amazed to see a striking building with a high sweeping roof in three ascending tiers.

In Bali the symbol of holiness is the mountain of Gunung Agung, the sacred 'Great Mountain' of Bali. Christians in Bali dared to take this image, not to worship the mountain but to worship God who created the mountain as the Psalmist expressed:

"I lift up my eyes to the hills -
from whence will my help come?
My help comes from the Lord,
who made heaven and earth. (Psalm 121:1)

According to Wayan Mastra, the spiritual leader of the Protestant Church in Bali, Balinese consider that the three gifts of nature - fire, water and fresh air - are connected with Gunung Agung: the fire of the volcano, the breeze of the mountain top and the fresh water of the volcanic lake.

At the Blimbingsari church one enters through the traditional split gateway which for traditional Balinese means the two halves of the great Himalayan Mt. Meru but for Christians in Bali means the sacred doorway or the way which invites us upwards. The sides of the doorway are decorated with a simple cross.

Once through the entrance gate one is guided by a stairway to the inner garden. In the usual Hindu temple, such a stairway would be guarded by fearsome figures but at this Balinese church the stairway is guarded by two kneeling angels in the posture of prayer. One finally enters the inner sanctuary and discovers a striking transformation.

Sunlight shines through the open pinnacle of the roof, Christian Church, Blimbingsari, Bali, Indonesia.

In a Bali Hindu temple there are many altars in the open air compound but in the sanctuary of Blimbingsari there is one single altar under the three-tiered roof. The sides of the

19

sanctuary are open to the garden to allow the breeze to come and go and through the open top of the tiered mountain-like roof the sky and sun are visible. Behind the single altar springs of water nurture tender lotus flowers. As the worship of the congregation proceeds accompanied by music from a traditional Indonesian gamelan orchestra, young girls in ceremonial sarongs present their offerings with delicate dance.

Here is a concrete example of the transformation of traditional culture into an indigenous and new expression of the Christian faith.

III Church in Community

The Church by the Street

The Church exists by the street. Many people pass by the church every day and the church stands silently as if without speaking. Yet the church is speaking day and night through its physical presence. It is like a pantomime without word, symbolically trying to convey its message. Job states, "The stranger has not lodged in the street; I have opened my doors to the traveller." (Job 31:32)

The open gate and open door of the Legian Christian Church, Bali.

In this sense, the shape and style of a church as seen from the outside by strangers is very important, as well as the design of the gate, the way of the approach, the door of the sanctuary and the decorations and designs of the outside walls. They deliver the message of the church around the clock to those who pass by. The church notice board and the symbol of the church usually stand outside the church and are of significance in the way they are integrated into the total structure of the church. They help to raise the consciousness of people and to extend an open invitation to strangers concerning the message and the programmes of the church.

The Search For Creative Indigenous Form

The question of which type and which outlook the church in Asia should take requires careful consideration among the members of the congregation, rather than relying upon architectural forms based on expediency.

I know of one congregation in Asia which discovered a gap in understanding between the architect's ideas and their own understanding of the kind of church they wanted so they changed to another architect. The final result was a very unique church which satisfied the members of the congregation. Of course, changing architects is not desirable but this case demonstrates the determination of that congregation to have the church building they desired.

One of the decisive issues to consider is whether the church looks foreign or 'other-worldly' or is in a style which will be more congenial and familiar to the people who live in the neighbourhood and pass by the church. It is not so much a question of whether one takes modern or classical style, since the indigenous spirit can be manifested through utilising modern technology.

Rev. Andrew Prasad in discussing church architecture in India made a valuable observation:

"The Reformed Churches right from the beginning committed the mistake of presenting Christianity as an 'other-worldly' religion. The indigenous architecture has taken much from the temple style, most probably in part to correct the inherited wrong tendency still dominating the Christian Church in India."[14]

It is obvious we need to give constant consideration to clarifying the Christian perspective and motivation as we involve ourselves in the search for new styles of church architecture in Asia.

The Internal Centre

Within the sanctuary one finds the centre which symbolically points to the meeting of time and eternity. This is the dwelling place of God and the heart of the Body of Christ. Traditionally, Orthodox churches have set aside the eastern end of the sanctuary as the most holy place. This is separated by the iconostasis, the partition with doors adorned with icons. There is an open door at the centre of the inconostasis through which the priest enters with the eucharist elements.

In traditional Catholic Churches the altar is placed at the end of the sanctuary, which is considered the most holy place and sometimes only the priest can have access to it. Protestant churches have reduced the separation between clergy and lay people by placing the communion table beside or in front of the pulpit to show that the preaching and the communion are both important sacraments of the church. According to each tradition, a particular place is the centre of worship in the arrangement of the sanctuary .

The church is the symbolic dwelling place of God, the meeting ground of time and eternity and it is not easy to create such a place. Genuine artistic creativity is required to actualise the theological understanding of the church. In this sense, the artistic use of the cross at the Church of Light in Ibaraki, Japan by architect Tadao Ando (see page 70) is a modern example of the interior centre of the sanctuary.

The Rhythm of Communion

Increasingly, we observe attempts among Protestant churches to make the communion table the central point of the sanctuary. Many Protestant churches now celebrate communion more frequently, partly due to theological and liturgical renewal of the meaning of holy communion and also partly due to the influence of the ecumenical movement. At ecumenical gatherings the eucharistic celebration brings people into a personal experience of the mystery and the agony of the faith in a deep and central way and many Protestants have come to acknowledge the one-sidedness of the pulpit-centred church.

We must acknowledge one important factor which has implication for the special arrangement of the sanctuary - which is that holy communion has two dimensions which come together to form a rhythmic movement.

One dimension is that we accept communion from God as the gift of Jesus Christ. With gratitude and thanksgiving we humbly receive the eucharist as the gift from the Lord, as the Lima study book states:

"The eucharist is a sacramental meal which by visible sign communicates to us God's love in Jesus Christ, the love by which Jesus loved his own 'to the end'." (John 13:1)[15]

The second dimension of the eucharist is the communion among God's people based on the communion from God. As we receive the gifts of God we share them among ourselves and on behalf of the whole creation. Holy communion is holy not only because it is the occasion of thanksgiving for the gift of God but also because it is the time to celebrate on behalf of the whole community the coming of the kingdom with the hope of restoration so that the life of cosmic circulation will be realised.

"The eucharist embraces all aspects of life. It is a representative art of thanksgiving and offering on behalf of the whole world. The eucharistic celebration demands reconciliation and sharing among all those regarded as brothers and sisters in the one family of God and is a constant challenge in the search for appropriate relationship in social, economic and political life. (Matt. 5:23f.; I Cor. 10:16f.; Cor. 11:20-22; Gal. 3:28)

"All kinds of injustice, racism, separation and lack of freedom are radically challenged when we share in the body and blood of Christ. Through the eucharist the all-renewing grace of God penetrates and restores human personality and dignity."[16]

How can this dual movement of communion be manifested visibly and symbolically in church architecture in Asia? What are the architectural reformations necessary in order to provide the kind of setting which will foster such circulation of holy communion?

Korean poet Kim Chi Ha, in his study on the Tong Hak peasants movement of the nineteenth century, discovered that they completely reversed the arrangement of the altar of their churches.

In the former period the peasants brought their fruits of labour to the altar table which was placed against the wall and the priest and congregation stood in front of it. But they changed the arrangement to place the table in the midst of the people so that after the thanksgiving all can share the fruits of labour in a circle. Kim Chi Ha commented on this reformation as follows:

"Whether we say Way, Truth or Life, they are not static abstract concepts but are always moving and constantly changing in circulation which is their substance. The peasants work in order to produce rice, which in turn gives vital life when it enters the human body through the mouth. Then the people, through having the vital power are able to work for the further production of rice.

"There is creative circulation of life through the people going out to engage in the work to produce rice and coming in to share the fruits of work together."[17]

Thanksgiving and Service

The rhythm of holy communion leads to the circle of thanksgiving and service. We offer thanksgiving for the gift of God. The word 'eucharist' (eucharistia) means 'to show thanks'. It is the public occasion when a community of God's people offer thanks for the love of God embodied in Jesus Christ. By receiving the body and blood of God we are sent out into the world in service to our neighbours in the world. It is the work of both personal and social diakonia to restore humanity and to renew the whole creation by bringing justice and peace.

How do we design our church structure to indicate this circle of movement of thanksgiving and service? What kind of imaginative symbols, what visible signs and creative colours and patterns will promote the dynamic interaction of thanksgiving and service?

IV The Church in Oikumene

Local and Universal

The church exists in a particular locality as the body of Christ but it does not exist in isolation. It is a part of the universal church. Many Asian churches are small in number, quite often in a situation of diaspora, dispersion. But they are, in their own way, a unique manifestation of the church universal. As we celebrate the eucharist in our local community we share the life of the church universal at all times and in all places.

To be ecumenical does not only mean participation in the unusual gatherings of Christians of different traditions in remote places like Geneva, Evanston or New Delhi. It begins with the place where we dwell as we recognise the presence of Christ who is the body of the church universal. St Paul's Catholic Church in Solo, Indonesia has universal designs of cup, fish and bread on the higher part of the interior wall to remind those present in worship of the universality of the church. (see page 98)

We need imaginative ways to express the universal reality of the church. In the chapel at Doshisha University in Kyoto, Japan a crown of thorns replaces the traditional cross. The symbol of the cross estranged from its original meaning is often used as the sign of crusading expansion of western nations or as a sentimental accessory or decoration. The chapel at Doshisha also acknowledges that the design of a crown of thorns has been used as the symbol of the liberation movement in Japan. We need such creative expressions of the church universal.

Unity in Diversity

To be universal does not mean to be conformist. Technology is universal but culture is local. To be ecumenical does not mean to abandon the cultural uniqueness of the local church. On the contrary, it encourages local unique cultural expressions of common faith in Jesus Christ. Today, internationalism does not mean homogeneous conformity nor modern westernisation. It means promoting a meeting ground for international learning about local identity expressed through local culture.

Diversity is an important component of the unity we seek. In our Christian faith, unity is the gift of God who is the only absolute with all others relative. With a humble spirit we bring our local cultural gifts to promote the possibility of engaging in international dialogue through the media of local cultural expression. The church, which is the body of Christ, is enriched by these diversified gifts.

In the realm of architecture, we notice the considerable impact of technology which has been associated for a long time with western culture. We need to uncover the creative use of this technology to foster indigenous expressions of the Christian faith.

Variety in Harmony

We have been thinking about the church as the body of Christ in a particular place. But we should also think in terms of the organic body in which the different parts join together to enable bodily function and growth. A key passage in the New Testament which deals with the image of body, describes it as follows:

"But speaking the truth in love, we must grow up in every way into him who is the head, into Christ, from whom the whole body, joined and knit together by every ligament with which it is equipped, as each part is working properly, promotes the body's growth in building itself up in love. (Ephesians 4:15-16)

Within a local congregation there are many different gifts endowed by God. It is the task of the minister to discover and train them and bring them together for joint team work so that each part is working properly and makes bodily growth.

Architectural work demands the joint activity of many disciplines. Building the church requires joint consolidation and cooperation of many trades and professional specialists such as artists, musicians, social workers, builders, painters, engineers, lawyers, nursery school teachers, designers, managers and, of course, the architect and minister. The task of building the body of Christ requires team work by gifted people who work together and bring their varied gifts in a spirit of unity.

The Church of Christ the King in Kurunagala, Sri Lanka, is one of the inspiring examples of the indigenous church in which we discern the contributions of various artists, craftsmen, sculptors and musicians helped by a sensitive minister and architect. (see page 44) This joint action is required as we try to combine the indigenous culture of different gifts with modern technology which also demands joint action of professional groups.

Response with the Whole Body

We have dealt with the unity and variety of the body of Christ from two points of view. One was the view of the ecumenical unity of the body of Christ as we recognise the significance of the local church within the church universal. The other was joint action within the body of Christ through team work and collaboration of various professional specialists required for the building of the church.

Now we come to the third dimension of the unity of the body in terms of the whole bodily response to God's gracious work at the time of worship. We participate in worship not only through oral expression but also through the visible expressions and through physical movement. We not only listen to the sermon but we also read the psalms and sing hymns. We not only see symbols like the cross but also bring signs of our thanksgiving to the altar. We participate in the worship as a whole body. We dedicate our body as a living sacrifice to God. (Romans 12:1)

In the Koganei Midori Church on the outskirts of Tokyo we see a special desk on the left side of the altar where ikebana (flower arrangement) is dedicated each week according to the theme of the Sunday service. (see page 68) In Orthodox churches incense is burned during the eucharist to promote the atmosphere of worship and to strengthen the spiritual communion. In churches in Indonesia and Thailand dance is frequently used as a means of expressing the Christian message. Fitting use of drama, pantomime, music and video are also very effective if they are well prepared.

During the service in the Protestant Church in Denpasar, Bali, the offering is presented with a traditional Balinese offering dance.

As we move towards the twenty-first century I believe there will be a radical change in the form and style of communication which will develop simultaneous use of all the senses of one's body. We need to raise the question of which kind of architectural arrangement will provide the ground to actualise a multidimensional means of communication and sharing in our church. But at the same time, we should not be too hasty to make superficial and artificial change. Instead we should find appropriate forms which are not strange to the community and which are deeply rooted in the Christian faith.

Small is Beautiful

Since modern architectural work usually demands a large scale of construction which in turn requires a bigger budget, we tend to conclude that the churches in Asia which are relatively small in number with limited resources may not be able to have a desirable church building. This is one of the underlying dilemmas of many Asian churches.

To what extent is financial capacity the determining factor in the choice of suitable architecture in Asia? Is it possible for a small congregation to construct their own house of God to fit their needs and context? Have we been more concerned with quantitative expansion rather than quality of expression? These are the questions which must be wrestled with continuously by each of us in our own context.

We have learnt from the experience of contemporary western society that the effort to be a great society does not necessarily result in a good society.[18]

Socrates is purported to have said that it is good to have close friends in a small house. Jesus remarked once, "For where two or three are gathered in my name, I am there among them." (Matthew 18:20)

It is told that Sen No Rikyu, the founder of the art of tea ceremony, stressed simplicity and ordinariness. He has set his tea ceremony in a space of four and a half tatamis square (approximately four square metres), including the tokonoma alcove in which to place the ornaments such as a hanging picture, flower arrangement and incense. There is meaning in the expression of the British economist Shumacher that "small is beautiful".[19]

I found such an example in a small church among the

working people's district along the hillside of Seoul. The space of the church is very limited yet inside the walls are painted with several pictures of the Exodus story depicted by a Minjung artist. Everyone took off their shoes and sat on the floor in a circle. The space was small but very warm in atmosphere. It was a congenial koinonia, a community of love and hope.

The bamboo church in the Philippines comes to me as another example. The chairs, wall, altar and even the musical instrument are all made from bamboo which symbolises the spirit of life. (see page 92) The church in Ibaraki by Tadao Ando (see page 70) built with a limited budget shows how imaginative creativity can produce a church which is small but beautiful. The permeating light of the cross which fills this small sanctuary symbolises that it is the house of God.

There is profound meaning in the promise of Christ who said, "Do not be afraid, little flock, for it is your Father's good pleasure to give you the kingdom." (Luke 12:32)

Concluding Reflection

We have made a brief survey of the issues and directions of Christian architecture in Asia and recognise that there is a variety of exciting new developments. In order to have steady creative development we need inter-disciplinary team work to build up the body of Christ in Asia. This will help us find the relevant form of the body of Christ to fit the Asian context, utilising both modern technology and Asian cultural tradition.

Such a project cannot be undertaken by an individual but demands the cooperation of various specialists based on the theological perspective of the church in Asia. Church building is one of the most corporate and comprehensive thanksgiving offerings to God. It demands a rather large budget and support and cooperation of the congregation with professionals, particularly talented creative architects.

No matter how well coordinated and artistically demonstrated, we must recognise that there is no final and absolute structural form. There is a limitation of human capacity, both corporate and personal and it is also true that our context is always changing and demands new creative endeavours to meet the challenge of each new day.

The work of church architecture contains an eschatological

dimension and the more we humbly recognise our limitations the more courageously we can engage in the task assigned to us. In this regard, it is important to have a sense of vocation.

It is appropriate that we publish this book when the Christian Conference of Asia is preparing for its Assembly in Colombo, Sri Lanka with the theme: "Hope in God in a Changing Asia."

Church architecture provides the structural embodiment of Christ. The church is the dwelling place of God and of the household of God and is a sign that we have hope in God in a changing Asia.

---

1 Paul Minear, Images of the Church in the New Testament, (1961) p.173.

2 Statement "Confessing the Faith in Asia Today", (East Asia Christian Conference, October 26-November 3, 1966) p. 51.

3 Ibid., p. 53-56.

4 EACC Hymnal, (East Asia Christian Conference, 1962).

5 Sound the Bamboo, (Christian Conference of Asia, 1990).

6 Masao Takenaka, (ed.) Christian Art in Asia (Kyo Bun Kwan in association with the Christian Conference of Asia, 1975).

7 Masao Takenaka and Ron O'Grady, (ed.) The Bible Through Asian Eyes (Pace Publishing in association with the Asian Christian Art Association, 1991).

8 Yasuyuki Takahashi, Yoshimasa Tsuchiya, Kyoshi Nagahisa, Tsuneaki Kato, Shin Nara and Kaname Iwai, (ed.) Kyokai Kenchiku (Church Architecture), (Kyodan Publishing, 1985)

9 Jyoti Sahi, "A Theology of Creation", Image (No.50, March 1992).

10 Concerning the meaning of space in Japanese architecture, see Kisho Kurokawa, Rediscovering Japanese Space (Weatherhill, 1988) also Mitsuo Inoue, Space in Japanese Architecture (Weatherhill, 1985).

11 Isaiah 11:6-9.

12 Richard Reinhold Niebuhr, "Being in Proportion: Jonathan Edwards' Philosophy of Excellency, in Streams of Grace, (Doshisha University Press, 1983).

13 Soetsu Yanagi, The Unknown Craftsman, A Japanese Insight into Beauty (1972) pp.109f.

14 Andrew Prasad, "Church Architecture in India: Borrowed and Indigenous".

15 William Lazareth, Growing Together in Baptism, Eucharist and Ministry, A Study Guide (World Council of Churches 1982) p.49.

16 Ibid, p.74.

[17] Kim Chi Ha, <u>Meshi to Katsujin</u> (Rice and the Living Person) (Ochanomizu Shobo, 1989) pp. 63-64 translated from the Japanese version to English by Masao Takenaka.

[18] Robert Bellah, Richard Madsen, William M. Sullivan, Ann Swidler, Steven M. Tipton, <u>The Good Society</u> (Alfred A. Knopf, 1991). In the introduction to the book the question is raised: "Is the great society a good society?" p.7.

[19] E.F. Schumacher, <u>Small is Beautiful</u>.

Note:

All Biblical quotations are from the New Revised Standard Version of the Bible, © Division of Christian Education of the National Council of the Churches of Christ in the United States of America, 1989.

The Place
Where God Dwells

An Introduction to
Church Architecture in Asia

Akapparambu Jacobite Church

Possibly from as early as 550 A.D. a Christian church known as 'Syrian' has existed in the south-west coast of India in the state of Kerala. It claims to have been founded by the Apostle St Thomas and derives its rite and traditions from the Jacobite church of Syria.

Akapparambu Jacobite Church, located in the village of Akapparambu, Kerala, has the characteristics of Syrian church architecture. It is said to have been built in the 10th century, although there is no documentation to substantiate this claim.

The front gate of Akapparambu Jacobite Church topped with three Syrian crosses.

Interior view of Akapparambu Jacobite Church. The highly-decorated altar glows from the light of candles and many small light bulbs.
The twelve candles represent the twelve apostles, with the cross of Christ in the central position. Signs of age are evident in the colourful wall paintings.

Side view, Akapparambu Jacobite Church, Kerala.

St Joseph Syrian Catholic Church, Akapparambu

St Joseph Syrian Catholic Church, Akapparambu, Kerala, is also believed to have been built in the 10th or 11th century and its architectural style has some similarities with the Akapparambu Jacobite Church. The worship area, which can accommodate approximately 100 people, is divided by partitions. The worshippers sit on the floor for services, with men sitting in front of the partitions and women and children occupying the rear area.

St Joseph's building was formerly a part of the Akapparambu Jacobite Syrian Church but a rift within the early church led to the establishment of a Roman Catholic Uniat body. The remainder of the Jacobite Church is divided between the Orthodox Syrian Church and the Mar Thoma Syrian Churches.

The approach to St Joseph Syrian Catholic Church, Akapparambu, Kerala.

The side altar,
St. Joseph Syrian
Catholic Church,
Akapparambu.

Interior view looking towards
the front altar of St. Joseph Syrian
Catholic Church, Akapparambu.

The Jebalayam of Kristukula Ashram

The Jebalayam (House of Prayer) of Kristukula Ashram, Tirupattur, Tamilnadu was consecrated on 9 June 1933, five years after work first began. It was founded by an Indian doctor, S. Jesudason, in cooperation with a British colleague, Dr. Ernest Paton. Both men had worked in the nearby hospital. The jebalayam is surrounded by a low parapet wall which can be used for seating. The floor of the worship area is covered with stone slabs and the worshippers sit on mats which can be rolled up after the service. The shrine is recessed within a large but non-functional vimana in keeping with Hindu tradition. This was an expense which the founders felt essential to express identification with the life of the neighbourhood. The exterior of the vimana carries many carvings but care was taken to avoid any imagery which could be regarded as being idolatry.

Front gopuram (gate tower) of Kristukula Ashram. Both front and rear gopurams are very highly decorated in the Dravidian temple style. A cross on each tower occupies the central position.

Carving on a door panel of the jebalayam of Kristukula Ashram. Wood carving is a tradition throughout India and there are many carvings of traditional religious symbols on the pillars and the walls of this building, as well as on the panels of the doors.

(below)
Interior view of the jebalayam of Kristukula Ashram, showing the altar. The worship area measures approximately 17 x 16 metres and is 13 metres in height. It is a mandapam style of pillared architecture, which provides a spacious area for congregational worship.

Saccidananda Chapel

The Saccidananda Chapel of the National, Biblical, Catechetical and Liturgical Centre of the Roman Catholic Church of India is located in St. Mary's Town, Bangalore. 'Saccidananda' literally means 'the blissful awareness of reality'.

Inspired by the Second Vatican Council, the Centre tries to embody the spirit and ideals of the church-in-renewal, including the basic aspect of indigenisation. According to the founder-director of the Centre, Fr. Amalorpavadass, "the whole campus of the Centre is a concrete witness to this indigenisation effort and as such is a synthesis of Indian Christian theology and spirituality."

The tiered roof and the shape of the building resembles a Dravidian temple (Southern India) plan combined with the basic structures of the Aryan fire altar (Northern India).

The grills of the front door and the fourteen windows of the chapel, designed by Jyoti Sahi, attempt to show the synthesis of Indian Christian spirituality. One of the window grills depicting the dancing Shiva was so controversial it was finally taken down and replaced with a descending dove to depict the Holy Spirit.

Regional Seminary Chapel, Orissa

The conical terraced roof of the Chapel of the Regional Seminary in Orissa, North India follows the form of early thatched shrines surmounted by the symbol of the vessel of life which is like a finial. A frieze representing dancing tribal people with offerings runs around the exterior walls of the hexagonal nave.

The circular rhythms of time and space in Asian spirituality and the more linear approach to history in the Bible are expressed in the structure of the church which combines a basic rectangular form with a circular, hexagonal central portion.

The tribal drum image, symbolising the primal word or sound, appears often inside the church.

Cathedral of Christ the Living Saviour

The Cathedral of Christ the Living Saviour was built by the Anglican Church of Sri Lanka on a central site in Colombo. The foundation stone was laid on 28 October 1968 and the completed building was consecrated by Rt. Rev. Cyril Abeynaike, Bishop of Colombo, on 7 November 1973, the 128th anniversary of the founding of the Diocese of Colombo.

The sanctuary, which seats 2000 people, is octagonal in shape to resemble a tent and has been kept simple and open. Designed by Mr. T.N. Wynne-Jones and Mr. P.H. Wilson Peiris, it incorporates principles drawn up by the clergy and laity of the diocese.

The floors slope downwards from the exits to the main altar so that bishop, priest and people are all seated at the same level. The communion table has been placed in a central position.

Side view of the main entrance, Cathedral of Christ the Living Saviour, Colombo.

Interior view of the Cathedral of Christ the Living Saviour, Colombo.

Cathedral Church of
Christ the King, Kurunagala

The Cathedral Church of Christ the King, Kurunagala, Sri Lanka took shape under the direction of Bishop Lakdasa de Mel, an Asian pioneer of indigenous art and the first Ceylonese to become a Bishop. Plans were drawn by architect P.H.WilsonPeiris and the building was completed in 1960.

The architecture is inspired by the Polonnaruwa period. The cement, brick, tiles and wood used are all products of SriLanka.

Exterior view of the Cathedral Church of Christ the King against the backdrop of Elephant Rock. The temple-like 100-foot tower is topped by a bronze cross. In keeping with Hindu tradition of 'vimana' the altar is placed within this highest part of the building.

The 14-foot figure of Christ the King on the east wall of the Cathedral Church of Christ the King. Beneath the figure a slab of local stone is inscribed with text in the Sinhala language commemorating the consecration of the sanctuary on 6 January 1956 by the Most Rev. Arabindo Nath Mukerjee. Also carved are symbols of sun and moon in keeping with local tradition. Important shrines in Sri Lanka are marked in this way as a sign that they should endure as long as sun and moon endure.

Looking towards the large hanging on the east wall of the Cathedral Church of Christ the King.

Jeushi Christian Church, Shantou

The Jeushi Christian Church in Shantou, China was founded in 1930 to commemorate the 70th anniversary of the arrival of the gospel in Jeushi, Shantou on the southern east coast region of Guangdong province.

Situated in an area of 1,100 square metres, with flowers and trees, it has a quiet and beautiful environment. The building was reconstructed for worship just prior to Christmas 1980 and the design incorporates both eastern and western styles.

**C
H
I
N
A**

Side view of the front entrance, Jeushi Christian Church, Shantou. The walls of grey stone and the white cement pillars complement the terracotta and green roof tiles.

The high vaulted ceiling of the Jeushi Christian Church, Shantou. Good acoustic design enables the speaker in the front of the building to be clearly heard throughout the hall without need of an amplifying system.

The front entrance of the Jeushi Christian Church resembles an ancient Chinese palace, with a main doorway set between two subordinate doors.

Yihu Church, Guangdong Province

The Yihu church is located in the Yihu village of Chaoan township, Caozhou city, Guangdong province.

First established in 1888, it was rebuilt in 1991. The five-storey building includes a bell tower which is actually an audio amplifier.

The church covers an area of 1,270 square metres and has a worship area of 680 square metres.

It was designed by the Chaozhou Municipal Design Institute.

Yihu Church,
Chaoan town,
Caozhou city.

48

Xianjiang Church, Ruian City

Xianjiang town is part of Ruian city which is situated on the east coast of Zhejiang province. Similar in style to the Mayu Church (see next page), the Xianjiang church is active in the Three-Self Patriotic Movement Committee and the Council of Churches in Ruian city.

Mayu Church, Ruian

The Mayu church was built on a small, exposed hill in Mayu town, Ruian city, Zhejiang Province, as recently as 1990. It covers an area of 1,000 square metres.

The bell tower of the church bears some similarity to a traditional Chinese pagoda but the cross which stands on top of the tower identifies the building as a Christian church.

Jishan Church, Minjing County

The Jishan Church of Minjing County stands in the Qianmian Village of Jishan township, Minjing County, Fujian Province. The church was built in 1919 but Christian activities were stopped in 1952. In 1984 reconstruction began. A small building, it fits well into the environment and uses a typical local building style. The picture below shows the church before restoration began but in spite of obvious deterioration the building's charm is apparent.

Churches of Lan Yu (Orchid Island)

Lan Yu (Orchid Island), which lies some 60 kilometres off the east coast of Taiwan, is home to several tribes of indigenous people who have incorporated traditional cultural symbols into their places of worship.

Yayu Village Presbyterian Church

Yayu Village on the west coast of Lan Yu is home to the Yami tribe who derive their livelihood from fishing. Their church has been built to represent the fishing boat (tatala) which is the basis of the people's livelihood.

Front entrance, Yayu Village Presbyterian Church. The motif centred above the front door is the symbol of the Presbyterian Church of Taiwan. A representation of a fishing boat can be seen either side of the door. On each side of the roof can be seen the "mata totala" (eyes of the boat).

Interior of the Yayu Village
Presbyterian Church, showing
the pulpit decorated with
the community's traditional
symbols of eyes, people and
waves. The large wall cross is
also highly decorated with traditional
patterns. Set on the wall alongside
the cross are symbols of moon
and stars which are of great importance
in the life of seafaring people, guiding them
through the darkness of night.

(below)
Section of the front wall of the Yayu Village
Presbyterian Church on which a boat is
painted. The symbol on the prow of the boat
represents a human being.
This symbol also appears on the stern and
on the sides of the boat between symbols of
waves. The pattern of the mata totala (eye)
of the boat is clearly visible on the boat
and higher up on the church wall above the
drawing of the boat.

(above)
Interior front wall, Imurua Village Catholic Church, showing the traditional fishing boat with symbols of the Yami people. The base of the marble altar is in the shape of a large fish, further reinforcing the affinity of the people with the sea.

Imurua Village
Catholic Church

Section of side wall, showing ornate carving which covers the entire interior of the church. The colourful and symbolic art is the work of three professional artists, Shappanndnuneewan, Shappannganruplee-an and Shappenmanukdwan.

Side wall, Ivarjunn Village Catholic Church, showing wooden slat windows open for ventilation and light. On the central panel the long instrument used for potato digging supports two of the traditional boats, with the top boat carrying the cross.

Ivarjunn Village Catholic Church

(below)
Back wall, Ivarjunn Village Catholic Church, decorated with the patterns of the Yami people of this district.

Street frontage of the
Wu-Tai Sacred Heart Church
which is the worship centre for
the Rukai Mansurusu tribe.
Construction of the building
began in 1961 and was
completed in 1963.
It is built from stone which
is a common material for
ordinary house construction.

Wu-Tai
Sacred Heart Church

Usually beside the house of the
tribal master there is a large stone
on which his name is inscribed.
The people at Wu-Tai have
followed that tradition and erected
a stone pillar beside the church.
On the base of the stone is a cross.
The inscription in Chinese calligraphy on the stone pillar translates
into 'Heavenly Lord's House'.

The front entrance of the Wu-Tai Church. On top of the bell tower is an ancient Nestorian cross.

Interior of Wu-Tai Church with seats facing the pulpit, the place for the master of the tribe. The chairs are built to represent the hero of the Rukai tribe. The arms of the chairs are painted to resemble the snake which is believed to give power to the tribe. The hat design on the top of the head of each chair symbolises the honour given to people who have made a distinctive contribution to the community. The chair beside the pulpit has additional decoration of clothes and jewellery to indicate that it is the seat of the master.

Christ Temple of Tao Fong Shan

The Christ Temple of Tao Fong Shan Christian Study Centre of Chinese Religion and Culture, Shatin, New Territory, Kowloon is an octagonal shaped building with decoration and details adapted and modified as Christian symbols.

The octagonal shape is intended to reflect the eight paths of Buddhism (Tao). The founder of the centre, Norwegian missionary Karl Ludvig Reichelt, gave the name Tao (the way or path) Fong (wind) Shan (mountain) to symbolise the Christian and Buddhist relationship. The architect of the temple was Johannes Prip-Miller, a Dane.

The altar with Christian symbolism is from Nanking, China. The baptismal font has a Chinese Nestorian cross (a cross on a lotus). The roof is traditional Chinese ceramic tiles. On its pinnacle is a cross. Statues of Biblical figures decorate the eight roof hips.

(right)
The bell of Christ Temple,
decorated with a Nestorian Cross.

(below)
View of the altar,
Christ Temple, Tao Fong Shan.

道成肉身

風隨意思而吹　　　道與上帝同在

Chinese Methodist Church

The distinctive Chinese style building of the Methodist Church in Hong Kong was constructed in 1936 at the junction of two main thoroughfares in Wan Chai, on the island of Hong Kong.

In 1984, centennial celebrations commemorated the founding of the Cantonese-speaking work begun in Hong Kong by eleven Chinese Methodist lay persons from Canton and Fatshan, China.

This church has now been demolished to make way for further development in the region.

A section of one of the side walls sloping in to the narrow back wall of Chinese Methodist Church, Wanchai.

The pagoda-style
tower on the rooftop
of the Chinese Methodist
Church, Wan Chai.

(below)
The main entrance
to the Chinese
Methodist Church,
Wan Chai.

St Mary's Church

St Mary's Catholic Church in Causeway Bay on Hong Kong island was built 50 years ago in the architectural style of a Chinese Buddhist temple with a central white cross indicating that this is a Christian church. The only record of the architect is that it was a Mr. Lam.

In 1981 to mark the 80th anniversary of the Catholic Church in Hong Kong, the building was completely renovated in the traditional Chinese colours of red, green and gold.

Looking up into the ceiling of St Mary's Church.

Front altar of St. Mary's Church, showing the stained glass window designed by a Chinese priest, Wong Po Lan. The calligraphy on the wooden panel below the window, just discernible above the altar table reads "holy, holy, holy".

Lutheran Theological Seminary

The Lutheran Theological Seminary, which was founded in 1913 in Hubei province, China, moved to Hong Kong in 1948.

Its new campus, situated on a hilltop in the New Territories, was dedicated in November 1992. The architect is Helena To of The Architects' Mission, Hong Kong.

Architecturally, the facility is conceived as a space for exploring the relationships between God and humanity. The chapel is geographically located at the highest level with all other buildings spiralling around it.

A 30-foot cross between the chapel and the academic wing dominates the scene. At the base of the cross, water flows from the centre of a large rock and meanders through a channel in the courtyard towards the library and classroom area.

The building style is patterned on the humble residential architecture of southern China, with whitewashed walls, clay tiles and black pitched roof throughout.

A view of the Lutheran Theological Seminary, looking towards the classrooms and the library wing.

The reflecting pool located in the centre of the classroom and library wing of the Lutheran Theological Seminary. The water flows into the pool by way of a narrow channel from the rock spring.

(below)
The main plaza of the Lutheran Theological Seminary. In the centre is the Ming Chieh chapel, to the left the dining hall and to the right conversation alcoves. The rock spring in the foreground rests at the foot of a 30 foot cross just out of the picture.

Episcopal Christ Church, Nara

The Episcopal Christ Church was founded in 1886 in Nara, the ancient capital city of Japan. It changed location several times before obtaining the present site in 1909. The first plan for the church was rejected by the missionary because it was too Japanese. The second plan was opposed by the government on the ground that it was too Western. Finally, the plans for the existing building were accepted and construction began in 1929 with the dedication cermony in April 1930.

The sanctuary is made of Japanese cypress (254 trees) which Yoshitaro Oki, the chief architect, obtained from the mountains of Yoshino and Wakayama. The basic style is basilica.

**J
A
P
A
N**

The main entrance to the Episcopal Church Nara is reached by climbing stone stairways of about 50 steps in total (as found in Buddhist temples in Japan). Centred above the doorway is a cross on a trinitarian symbol.

The central communion table, the cross, candlesticks and flower vases of cloisonne ware are the work of various professionals who have fashioned them in the craft style of the Tenpyo (Nara) period.

Interior of Episcopal Christ Church, Nara looking towards the front altar. Sliding paper screens (shoji) on both sides of the sanctuary allow for natural light.

In 1919 the congregation planted 100 small paulownian saplings in the church grounds as an act of peace to mark the conclusion of World War 1. The trees were used in the building of the main chancel.

Koganei Midori-cho, United Church of Christ

Koganei, a suburb north-east of Tokyo, retains some vegetable fields which provide a rural atmosphere for the Koganei Midori-cho church.

A granite pathway through bamboo bushes leads to the heavy wooden entrance doors. Once inside the building there is a flat space where worshippers remove their shoes in keeping with the Japanese custom on visiting a home.

The interior design incorporates paper sliding windows (shoji) on either side of the sanctuary, permitting soft natural light. The floor of the central altar is supported on cedar pillars which rest on stone signifying Christ as the cornerstone of the house.

A simple wooden cross is centred on a wall of cream-coloured rice paper which has a design of pine trees symbolising everlasting life. The communion table is centred below this cross, between the pulpit and a stand bearing an ikebana (flower) offering.

A small congregation was formed by Rev. Keiichi Yamamoto during 1965 and 1966. Mr Hirokuni Taniguchi, Professor of Architecture at Tokyo Polytechnic University, designed the building which was dedicated in April 1970.

Interior of the Koganei Midori-cho church, looking towards the front altar.
The Japanese sense of simplicity and space is maintained throughout the worship area.

Looking towards the entranceway of Koganei Midori-cho.

Church of the Light, Ibaraki

The Church of the Light is located in a quiet residential street in the district of Ibaraki, Osaka. It consists of a rectangular area sliced through at a fifteen-degree angle by a completely freestanding wall that separates the entrance from the chapel. Light penetrates the profound darkness of this box through a cross cut into the altar wall.

The architect, Tadao Ando, has used natural materials for parts of the building that come into contact with a hand or foot because he says "it is essentially through the body that we are aware of architecture. Materials such as wood or concrete which have substance, communicate this sense to the worshippers who come into contact with the wood and the concrete in this building."

"Openings have been restricted because light shows its brilliance only against the backdrop of darkness. Nature's presence is limited to the element of light and rendered abstract. Through responding to such abstraction the architecture grows purer.

"The floor and pews are made of rough scaffolding planks which are low cost and well suited to the character of the space."
- Tadao Ando

Exterior view,
Church of the Light,
Ibaraki,showing the
building's strong clean lines.

"The linear pattern formed by
reflection of the rays of the sun,
a migrating cross of light, expresses
man's relationship with nature."
- Tadao Ando

Church on the Water, Hokkaido

A plateau in the central mountains of Hokkaido, Japan's coldest region, is the setting for this chapel. Nearby are areas of thick wilderness. The entire region is blanketed in green from spring to summer and then transforms in winter to an unbroken expanse of white.

The chapel consists of overlapping squares erected on the shore of an artificial pond which was created by diverting a nearby stream. A free-standing L-shaped wall wraps around the back of the building and one side of the pond.

"Entry to the church is from the back and involves a circuitous route along the free-standing wall. The murmur of water accompanies one's progress but its source remains hidden, heightening expectations, until one confronts the broad expanse of the pond. Making a 180-degree turn, one ascends a gentle slope to enter a glass-enclosed vestibule, a box of light.

"Arriving in the chapel, one again confronts the pond whose placid expanse and large cross rising from the water are visible through the glass altar wall." - Tadao Ando.

The overlapping squares of the Church on the Water, Hokkaido.

(above) Looking out from inside the Church on the Water in the stillness of winter.

"The entire glass wall can slide to the side, opening the church to the pond which exists purely in its wilderness setting. The sound of water, the fragrance of trees, the song of birds - here people encounter nature directly." - Tadao Ando.

(below) Looking out from inside the Church on the Water in summertime.

Christian Theological Seminary Chapel, Tokyo

The Christian Theological Seminary Chapel is part of the Tokyo Christian College and University which is situated at the southern edge of Chiba New Town, south east of Tokyo. The chapel is located at the heart of the campus and was designed by Arata Isozaki Architectural Atelier (studio) and dedicated in 1989.

Interior view, looking to the altar, chapel of the Christian Theological Seminary.

74

The rounded roof structure of the Chapel of the Christian Theological Seminary combines with circles of lights to form a dramatic pattern around the simple white cross on the altar wall. The chapel expresses the spirit of harmony and the virtues of faith, hope and love.

(below):
Exterior view of the Chapel of the Christian Theological Seminary, showing the three round roofs which are covered by slate on concrete reinforcing. Its modern appearance seems to contain both the classical tradition of Byzantine and the Oriental circular style

Yichon Dong Presbyterian Church

The Yichon Dong Presbyterian Church in Seoul, Korea combines both Gothic and Basilica styles and stands in contrast with the Catholic Church alongside which is built in Korean style.

Inside the Presbyterian Church each pair of windows is set within an arch and centred in each arch is a Christian symbol. Those on the left side of the building represent stories from the Old Testament and those on the right are stories from the New Testament. Shown opposite is the dove sent out by Noah, returning with an olive branch.

The wooden exterior doors are decorated with metal fish symbolising Jesus Christ and vines representing Christianity. Above the main door is a 'victory' symbol; the central symbol on the side doors indicates joy and the symbol on the pillar alongside the doors derives from Buddhist culture.

Kanghwa Anglican Church

Anglican missionaries arrived in Korea in 1890 and moved into the Kanghwa area near Inchon. Set on a hill, the Kanghwa Anglican Church was built in 1893 following the traditional architectural style of a Korean Confucian temple, with the main building situated in the centre of a compound. In 1980 the church complex was declared an important cultural asset. The architect was a Korean, name unknown.

Front entrance, Kanghwa Anglican Church.

78

Corner of exterior
roof structure,
Kanghwa Church
decorated in traditional
Korean style.

(below)
Exposed beams of the
interior roof structure,
Kanghwa Church.

Taejon Diocese

The earliest churches in Korea were nearly all built in the style of Confucian temples. A few are very fine examples and have been made cultural assets. To build in this style now is too costly; even repairs are difficult and expensive to carry out. Consequently, a number of original style churches have been replaced with modern brick and concrete buildings.

Shown here are four churches in the Taejon Diocese which were built in Confucian style and all are still in use today.

Chung Chong Nam-Do, Pudaedong, Chonan city (below) was consecrated on November 4 1920, the Pyongchon Church (top, opp.) was consecrated on November 6 1921 and the Eumsong Church (centre, opp.) was consecrated October 7 1923.

Consecrated on October 16 1923, the Chinchon Church (bottom, opp.) was threatened by a plan for new roading which would pass right through the site on which the church stood. Local government decided the church must be preserved and the entire community, not just Christians, collected enough money to move the church and re-site it in the centre of the compound.

Chung Chong Nam-do, Pudaedong, Chonan city.

(above)
Side view,
Pyongchon
Church.

(left)
Side view,
Eumsong
Church.

(below)
Chinchon
Church.

Church of Christ in Thailand

The Church of Christ in Thailand (CCT) is the result of the joining together of Protestant churches in Thailand to present a united witness to the people.

Bumrungtum Church in Nakhom Pathom (below), designed by a Chinese architect, was opened in 1962 by the Disciples Christian Church.

First Church, Chiangmai (featured opposite) also has Disciples origins. Like other Disciples churches, it is now part of the CCT and is known in Chiangmai as the Community Church.

Bumrungtum Church, Nakhom Pathom.

Interior view of the Community Church, Chiangmai, looking towards the front altar which duplicates the tiered construction of the ceiling.

View of front entrance, Community Church, Chiangmai.

Payap University Chapel, Chiangmai

The chapel is the spiritual centre of Payap University, the first accredited school of higher education of the Church of Christ in Thailand.

The chapel was completed in September 1984 and dedicated during the 18th General Assembly of the Church of Christ in Thailand, hosted by Payap University.

The interior of the chapel is constructed almost entirely in teakwood. The furniture and chapel doors carry carvings in traditional Thai design.

Each carving contains a symbol which relates to the gospels, such as shepherd's staff, lilies, fish, loaves, bread.

(above)
Interior view, looking upward
through the glass spire,
Payap University Chapel.

The arched roof-line
and central spire of the
Payap University Chapel.

Bangkok Christian College Chapel

Founded by the Church of Christ, Thailand, Bangkok Christian College is a college for boys.

In its outward appearance, the chapel has a resemblance to Noah's ark and is based on the Chinese calligraphy for person.

The Chapel, Bangkok Christian College, Bangkok.

Church of the Holy Redeemer, Bangkok

The Church of the Holy Redeemer, situated in Soi Rum Rudi, Bangkok caused some controversy when it was built in the style of a Buddhist temple. Even the altar reflects the format of altars used in Buddhism. Today, the architecture is more accepted within one section of the Thai church.

(above)
Front altar,
Church of the Holy Redeemer,
Bangkok.

One of the side altars,
Church of the
Holy Redeemer,
Bangkok.

Sto Nino de la Paz Chapel

The Sto Nino de la Paz Chapel, also known as the Greenbelt Lagoon Chapel in Makati, Manila, uses glass and concrete sculptures to striking effect. The circular garden was designed by architect Enrique Dizon and artist Ramon Orlina designed the sculptures in glass and concrete.

The 10 metre high concrete and glass sculpture at the entrance to the chapel has the cross enclosed by two hands in what the artist, Orlina, calls a 'mudra' gesture (creating an enclosed space).

The entrance, Sto Nino de la Paz Chapel is dominated by the concrete and glass sculpture.

T
H
E

P
H
I
L
L
P
I
N
E
S

Tabernacle altar made of large emerald-green block of sculptured glass,
topped with a narra-wood table, Sto Nino de la Paz Chapel, Makati.

Looking across the garden area towards the interior of Sto Nino de la Paz Chapel, Makati.

Dambanang Kawayan (Fishermen's Chapel)

Dambanang Kawayan, the fishermen's chapel in Tipas, Tagig Rizal, Metro Manila, the Philippines was built in 1968. It is a Roman Catholic church and the architect was Fr. Ben Villiote. Like the ceiling, the altar floor and the altar furniture are all made from bamboo. The exterior walls of the church are concrete and the roofing is corrugated iron.

(opposite, top)
Section of ceiling, Dambanang Kawayan,
showing the pattern of the woven bamboo.

(opposite, below)
A portion of the bamboo staves which
line the walls of the Dambanang Kawayan.

View of the interior of Dambanang Kawayan looking towards the altar.

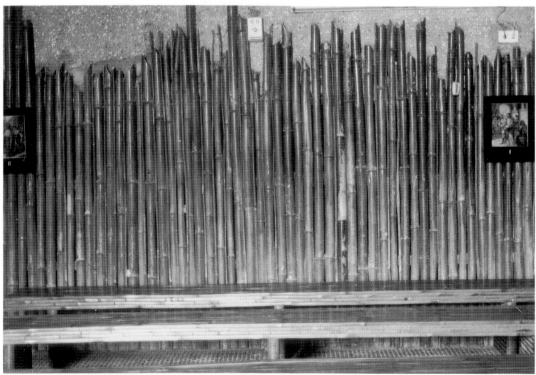

Dambanang Bayan (Bamboo Chapel)

Dambanang Bayan (Bamboo Chapel) in Punta St Ana, Metro Manila was designed by Fr. Ben Villiote and members of the the church. Built in 1950, it utilises bamboo for its fittings.

Bamboo Chapel, Punta St. Ana, Metro Manila.

EDSA Shrine of Mary

The Shrine of Mary stands at a busy intersection on the Epifanio de los Santos Avenue (EDSA) in Manila, Philippines. It was built to commemorate the 1986 people's revolution and stands at the site where the people gathered. The statue of Mary by Virginia Navarro towers above the chapel building, dominating the immediate landscape.

EDSA Shrine of Mary, Manila.

Chapel of the Holy Sacrifice

The Chapel of the Holy Sacrifice is the Catholic chapel at the University of the Philippines, Quezon City. Father Delaney, the priest for the Catholic student community, wanted it to reflect the ideas of youth so for architect he chose 25-year-old Leandro V. Lacsin, for structural engineering Alfredo L. Juinio and lighting was the task of Jose Segovia. The contractor was David Consunji who participated in planning to fit the low budget.

The round design was chosen to give a feeling of community participation in the Mass with the separation of choir and congregation completely eliminated. The ceiling of the dome was left undecorated to lend itself to dramatic use of coloured lights for various services.

The church was formally inaugurated on December 20, 1955.

Church of the Risen Lord

The Church of the Risen Lord, the Protestant chapel in the grounds of the University of the Philippines in Quezon City, Metro Manila, Philippines, utilises a welcoming arch form in its architecture.

Front entrance, Church of the Risen Lord, University of the Philippines, Quezon city.

Trinity Theological College Chapel

The chapel of Trinity Theological College, Mt. Sophia, Singapore incorporates the Chinese character 'ren'- (person) in its roof structure. The two strokes forming the character are unequal in length, symbolising the continuing search for God. The cross is placed between these two strokes to emphasise its theological significance and centrality to the gospel.

The walls of the building are Chinese handmade bricks taken from 'old No. 7', one of Mt. Sophia's first buildings which once stood on the site of the present chapel. The floor is of Cocciame tiles which are broken jagged pieces of marble symbolic of the jig-saw puzzles of life.

The long communion table, made from an old tree trunk of Chenghai wood, enables the Christian community to share the emblems together and the chancel, which is only six inches above the floor, has been designed to bring the communicant as near as possible to the celebrant. Architect for the project was Mr. Edwin Chan. The building was completed and dedicated in 1969 on the occasion of the 20th anniversary of the College.

SINGAPORE

Side view of the roof structure of Trinity Theological College Chapel, Singapore.

(below)
Interior view, Trinity Theological College Chapel, showing the front altar with glass window behind and roof beams which follow the line of the Chinese character for person. The stained glass panels at the front and back of the chapel continue the concept of people and God related through the cross. The warm colours of yellow, orange and light brown signify God's radiating power and hospitality. The different-sized discs of green, blue, purple and dark brown represent humanity.

St Paul's Church, Solo

St Paul's Roman Catholic Church is situated in Kerten, Solo on the island of Java, Indonesia. The exterior features Indonesian elements in its basic design while inside the building is decorated with symbols of the fish, cup and bread which have universal significance for Christians.

Exterior view of St. Paul's Church, Kerten. The wide sweep of the roof with its central peak resembles a large tent to remind the worshippers that they are pilgrims on a journey.

Interior view of St. Paul's Church, Kerten showing the stylised pattern of universal Christian symbols on the rafters of the ceiling: the bread and cup (representing communion) the fish (symbol of Jesus) and 'Chi Rho' derived from the first two letters of the Greek word for Christ.

Evangelical Protestant Church of Timor, Kalabahi, Alor.

The church built for the Pola congregation of the Evangelical Protestant Church of Timor (GMIT), Kalabahi, Alor, Indonesia, intentionally incorporates symbols which have historical meaning for Christians.

The architect was Marten Bella and the design was the work of Rev. S.L. Oiladang; both are Alorese. Building began in 1974 and the church was consecrated August 5, 1984.

The foundation of the church is in the form of a cross. The four wings of the building represent the four corners of the earth; they also represent the four directions from which Christians came to Alor: from the west (Holland), east (Moluccas), north (Manado, North Sulawesi) and south (the islands of Timor, Roti and Sawu).

To symbolise that the gospel is not closed to anyone, the eaves of each wing are 'open-ended'.

Front entrance and steeple, Pola church, Kalabahi, Alor. The base of the steeple tower takes its shape from the ordinary Alorese living quarters. The upper portion of the steeple tower to its peak represents a finger pointing upward. In the theological understanding of the indigenous religion, this shape indicates that everything in the world originates from above and will finally return to the place from which it came.

Christian Church, Blimbingsari

The church at Blimbingsari is regarded as the mother church of Bali, for Blimbingsari village is the place where the first Christian community was established in 1939.

The present church was begun in 1976 after an earthquake devastated it predecessor. It was the first to be built in indigenous style. The ebony shingle roof ascends in three distinct tiers to represent the mountains which hold special significance for Balinese people.

Entry to the church, which has no windows, walls or partitions, is through a traditional split gateway. Set on a hill, the new building was completed in 1981 and dedicated on November 11 of that year to commemorate the fiftieth anniversary of the Christian Church in Bali.

Seated facing the communion table, worshippers look through the open sides of the building (see opposite) to a spring of water running through a tropical garden.

Front view of the Christian Church, Blimbingsari.

Side view of Christian Church, Blimbingsari, showing the inner gate.

Christian Church, Denpasar

The Christian Church at Denpasar, Bali is built according to the traditional Balinese tripartite division which for Christians equates to the Trinity. This also represents the three God-given essential elements for life - air, water and fire. The floor and roof are both built on three levels.

The tiered roof resembles the wings of a bird which protect its young. They symbolise the protection which God gives.

Front view of the tiered roof of the church with central cross and logo designed by Nyoman Darsane.

Interior of Christian Church, Denpasar, looking towards the altar.
Behind the communion table is a traditional temple gate with a cross in the opening
representing Jesus as "the way, the truth and the life".

Front entrance,
Kwanji Christian
Church, Bali.

Other
Christian
Churches
in Bali

(below)
Padang Luis
Christian Church, Bali.

Abianbase Christian
Church, Bali.

(below)
Legian Christian
Church, Bali.

Photos

Thanks to all who provided photographs for this publication. We regret that in some instances the name of the photographer is not known so cannot be acknowledged.

We gratefully acknowledge the following persons whose generous contribution of photographs has made this book possible.

Jose Adang

Tadao Ando

Ken Hassall

Akio Kojima

Alison O'Grady

Ron O'Grady

Judo Poerwowidagdo

Masao Takenaka

Gillian Taylor

Megumi Yoshida

List of Churches

Index of Churches (contd)

Related Publications on the Arts in Asia

Painting and Sculpture:

CHRISTIAN ART IN ASIA , Masao Takenaka (now out of print)

THE BIBLE THROUGH ASIAN EYES, Masao Takenaka & Ron O'Grady
(available from the Christian Conference of Asia or Pace Publishing)

FRANK WESLEY, Exploring Faith with a Brush, Naomi Wray
(available from Pace Publishing or the Christian Conference of Asia)

Music:

THE EACC HYMNAL, D.T. Niles (now out of print)

SOUND THE BAMBOO, James Minchin, I-to Loh & Francisco Feliciano
(available from the Christian Conference of Asia)

Magazine:

IMAGE is the quarterly magazine of the Asian Christian Art Association. Now in its sixteenth year of publication it is a small illustrated up-date on recent Christian art in Asia. Includes news of art and artists in the region. (Subscription information available from the Asian Christian Art Association. For address see front of book.)